No, More Nonsense!

Limericks, Limericks,
and more Limericks

Fox, Fox,
and more Fox

Copyright © 2020 C. Fox, T.J. Fox, & T.L. Fox
All rights reserved.

ISBN: 979-85-76572-94-6

Dedication

For Amy. Thanks for picking up.
- C. Fox

To everyone that I do love
Here on Earth and up above
It's no rumor
We all need humor
And limericks I think the world of
- T.J. Fox

In memory of mother, who always enjoyed a good laugh.
- T.L. Fox

Table of Contents

Introduction: What is a Limerick? 1
A Boisterous Bakery 2
    Add Salt to Taste..3
    Hey, it's for a good cause… 4
    It's bad to fall flat… 5
    It's hip to dip! 6
    Chocolate Chip Confidence 7
Freaky Foods..11
    Prankfurters 12
    Cruel Gruel 13
    Hope there's gravy… 14
    Practically Pickled Peccary 15
    That's one way to lose weight… 16
    Gosh, a local specialty!...17
    Mind the Teeth!..18
    I sure am glad they figured out "cherry"................................19
    Trade you for mine? 20
    I Dig the Pig 21
    Lose Weight the Easy Way..22
What a Workday!...23
    Troubled Trucker 24
    Bassoon Monsoon..25
    Should've asked for help… 26

Billable Skills	27
Smiles are integral to good grades	28
Cerebral Circuitry	29
True That	30
Mind your P's!	31
Ruth's Truths	32
A Case for Ace	33
Not So Square	35
Blundered Plunder	36
Ewe Ought to Know Better	37
A Cast of One	38
She took her self-defense course seriously!	39
Rick's Tricks	40
A map to the kitchen, please	41
Ace Returns	42
Conductive Conduct	45
A trick (or more) from Sycamore	46
Hanky-Panky Boogie	47
Travel Time	48
A slow boat to Thailand	49
30,000 Feet of Shuteye	50
No one else is holdin' back…	51
I bet the apples won	52
Well, it's just one city within the region, OK?	53

    GP-Guess 54

    Wacky Waltzers 55

    Hope they like the cold… 56

    Quintilla Jocosa 57

Reading, 'riting, 'rithmetic 58

    Rhetorical Ramblings 59

    Shhhh… 60

    At least it's polite… 61

    Keep at it 62

    A few dollars and no sense 63

    This limerick intentionally left blank 64

    Got your words wrong 65

    Just don't cackle too loudly 66

Family Matters 67

    Wah-Wah-Wah 68

    They must've moved a lot… 69

    Uncouth Youth 70

    Dads of Lads 71

    The Prices of Crises 72

    Reflections on Life 73

Gaming the System 77

    No more Mr. Nice Guy 78

    You might try developing it earlier 79

    Losers have easier cleanup! 80

    Maybe she should switch to SCRABBLE............................81
    SCRABBLE can be tough, too!...82
    Then there's a triple-letter score on that 'Z'.......................83
    Go big AND go home…..84
Celebrities and Characters..85
    But they're all good at 'Family Feud'....................................86
    Pronounce it like the Queen…..87
    Mixed Massages 88
    Fear of Missing Out 89
    A Treat to Meet..90
    Dig Your Own Party Favor 91
    Capricious Crockett..92
    Wardrobe Malfunction..93
    Never Lend Livestock 94
    Late Night...95
Holidazed...96
    Hate to be his dentist…..97
    Counting Calories, Count? 98
    Holy Matri-moly 99
    Just don't sleep through dessert!..101
    Waiting out a winter wonderland… 102
    A hemisphere not far from here…......................................103
    Why not set the bar lower? 104
    Better lend him a scarf!...105

Nothing says "love" like an orbital sander............106

Who invited them anyway?............107

Peal the Bells............108

Madcap Menagerie............109

Peculiar Pelican't............110

Please don't laugh at my calf............112

Your wipers will just make it worse............113

Priorities are important!............114

Bet that crown slows him down............115

Too bad it wasn't a Beatle............116

Crooked Croc............117

Hope there was mint jelly............118

The 'wash in Oshkosh............119

Can't teach an old hog new tricks............120

Pondering Porkchops............121

But I bet it tastes 'lighter'............122

Eight arms can work a lot of fryers!............123

Amphibian Refreshment............124

Hop to it!............125

Before the show are the pre-moos............126

Should've got a running start............127

Sharing is Caring............128

DIY Lawncare............129

Early to bed............130

    This zoo has a museum, too. 131
    But can it moo-ltiply? 132
Passing the Bar 133
    O'Malley's Sallies 134
    Sleep Deep 137
Bonus Content 139
    A Request for the Reader 140
    More Books by these Authors 141

Introduction: What is a Limerick?

A limerick is a funny poem of five lines. The first, second, and fifth lines are longer and share a rhyme; and the third and fourth lines are shorter and share different rhyme. A limerick has a bouncy rhythm and usually ends with a joke.

Here's a taste:

A limerick has only five lines
Though it bears other telltale signs;
Chiefly its crimes
Are obnoxious rhymes
And a punchline that earns groans and whines

Often these five lines stand on their own, although many of our limericks have multiple stanzas and a common theme. Some of our favorites in this book tell a complete story from start to end.

We can't promise this book won't elicit any scoffs or eye rolls, though we hope you find a few genuine laughs within its pages.

A Boisterous Bakery

Add Salt to Taste

A fresh pretzel, named Misses McNalty
Who thought her flavor was faulty
Yelled to her baker
"Retry your shaker!"
The baker cried: "Hey - Don't get salty!"

Hey, it's for a good cause...

Diets are like sweet-tooth droughts
Temptation can bring weight-loss doubts
I can't help but wince
When I order Thin Mints;
My diets fail due to Girl Scouts

It's bad to fall flat...

A fresh fortune cookie named Wong
Sobbed aloud to some lonesome song
The cause of the drama?
He missed his momma...
She'd just been "a wafer" too long!

It's hip to dip!

I rarely snack on Pfeffernusse
But whenever I do, I sluice
That is to say dunk
Every last chunk
In my tea, coffee, or apple juice

Chocolate Chip Confidence

A cookie (who wasn't no dummy)
Had a doctor examine his tummy
And although his hips
Contained several "chips"
He mostly felt all cold and crummy

"For one of your condition and ilk"
Said the doctor, with voice smooth as silk
"I advise we treat
With a gentle heat
Then a soak in a bath of cold milk"

Before treatment was due to begin
Doc's intent was betrayed by a grin
His stethoscope-d torso
Would be trustworthy (moreso)
Were it not for the rumbling within

And his words had seemed salutary
But the cookie felt need to be wary
To heed the warning
Dad gave that morning:
"To beware the dangers of dairy"

That day he heard many a tale
Of brimstone, fire, and hail;
Pain and heartache
So strong it would make
A golden-brown biscuit go pale

"Many perils await baked goods today;
Consider the mocha or cafe au lait
Then some dubious folks
Would trick, trap, or hoax
You to rest on their platter or tray

Of survival, our duty's most hallowed
Precaution above all must be followed
From lyin' and cheatin'
Comes cookies - eaten!
Tasted... and chewed up... then swallowed!

Though milk looks enticing and creamy"
Echoed dad's voice, so dreamy,
"Remember our friend
Who met her end
Once she dunked in a latte so steamy?

And notice the way my brow wrinkles
To recall those poor chocolate crinkles...
Whose unscrupulous medic
Gave them all anesthetic
And they woke up afflicted with sprinkles!

And don't discount uncle biscotti
Last seen near a big mug of hot tea
Times they are bleak!
For it's over a week
And the cops still can't find his body!

So to this I ask your adherence:
Use caution and perseverance
I dread so the thought
Of the espresso shot
That follows your swift disappearance"

Thinking on this paternal demand
One could see the doctor had planned
To outwit and devour
Him within the hour
It was high time to make a stand

With all courage the cookie could pluck
He shouted a noise like a duck
"Doc, you're a quack!"
Began his attack
"Your ethics have all gone amuck

The saliva that rests on your lip
Shows the purpose of that milky dip
Don't you pull the wool!
I saw that drawer full
Of fudge sauce and dairy whip"

At that the cookie said no more,
Jumped up, and ran out the door
The doc was stranded
Hungry! Empty-handed!
And he'd failed as never before

By rebuking that smooth doctor's charm
The cookie never came to harm
Had he chose to go
Along with the flow
He surely would have bought the farm

For the odds...go ask your bookie!
With those little steps he took, he
Averted disaster;
And was fate's master...
After all, he was one smart cookie

Freaky Foods

Prankfurters

A mischievous miss named Bella
Played a practical joke on her fella;
When fixing his waffle
Did something awful;
Spread Vegemite in place of Nutella

But how young Bella was flustered
Once her fella served up lemon custard
And how she looked hurt!
When her favorite dessert
Had been swapped for hot English mustard

Cruel Gruel

The intrepid Ms. Mary Lou Micken
Makes a rare form of stewed chicken
With mushrooms and leeks
She stirs for two weeks
With a dash of cement mix; to thicken

Hope there's gravy...

A chef in dear Albuquerque
Has a famous recipe for turkey
Roast it at 507
'Til it smokes to high heaven
So the texture is not unlike jerky

Practically Pickled Peccary

A line cook in old New York
Deep fries a new type of pork
So coated in oil
It won't ever spoil
And so slick it won't stick to your fork

That's one way to lose weight...

My nutritionist caused quite a riot
By inventing the Brussel sprout diet
He's sure it will work
But there's one little quirk
He'll never convince me to try it

Gosh, a local specialty!

A diner down in Oshkosh
Has a pot that they never wash
With cultures of mold
That are key, I am told
To the taste of their spaghetti sauce

Mind the Teeth!

A sous chef in Kissimmee
Cooked up a great fricassee
With cheese off the grater
And jaw of alligator
Oh please won't you save some for me?

I sure am glad they figured out "cherry"

The original flavor of Popsicle
Faced just one major obstacle:
Who'd want to eat
Any icy treat
That tastes like flaming hot pickle?

Trade you for mine?

There was a young Greek lad named Spiro,
Who at lunchtime was eating a gyro,
He said, as he ate,
"This isn't so great,
I'd rather be eating a Hero!"

I Dig the Pig

My knees weak, they won't stop from shakin'
In my stomach and soul there's an achin'
What's best to treat
My ailment is meat
You know the one I mean - bacon

Lose Weight the Easy Way

Those watching their calories
Will enjoy diet tips such as these
For lunch that can't miss
Try the ol' "ham and swiss"
It's less fat, 'cause there's holes in the cheese!

What a Workday!

Troubled Trucker

A trucker from Minnesota
Had trouble meeting his quota
He should have gone right
But left was his plight
And he ended up in North Dakota

Bassoon Monsoon

A young man who played the bassoon
Had trouble remaining in tune
He said: "A new reed,
Is just what I need!"
And practiced all morning till noon

Should've asked for help...

A hunter shopped at J. C. Penny
Seeking pants, and while they had many
He did not succeed;
Camouflage was his need
He looked hard, but couldn't see any

Billable Skills

A dentist liked using her drill,
And found all the teeth she could fill,
She then used a file,
To improve each one's smile,
And included it all in the bill!

Smiles are integral to good grades

A Calculus teacher named Lyle,
Passed out the blue books in style,
He said, "Do your best,
On today's written test,"
And ended his talk with a smile!

Cerebral Circuitry

There was an old teacher named Max
Who graded the homework in stacks
When his brain shorted out
He was able to shout:
"At last I can truly relax!"

True That

A crafty old teacher named Fox,
Kept all of his notes in a box,
He said, through the tears,
"I have taught all these years,
But it's better than getting the pox!"

Mind your P's!

A Pirate was in quite a state
He was angry with his first mate
When they went to sea
His mate stole a "P"
Which left him, quite simply, "irate"

Ruth's Truths

A dentist was robbed by Mrs. Ruth
She was caught by a photo booth
"Not guilty!" she claimed
But the judge proclaimed:
"We want the tooth and nothing but the tooth"

A Case for Ace

The once was a sleuth named Ace
A detective, young and full of grace
With surplus resolve
Any case he could solve
Every challenge surely embraced

A young blond asked Ace for a meeting
She was sure her husband was cheating
She said as she cried:
"I'm sure that he lied!
There's some other woman he's tweeting!"

So enticed by her pretty face,
Ace was happy to take the case.
"I have a plan
To expose the man
And make sure he ends in disgrace!"

Now the hubby was all too clever
He never left clues… well, hardly ever
So Ace, on a hunch
Followed him to lunch
Which was a beneficial endeavor

Ace saw him meet an attractive gal
Who was clearly more than a pal
They soon made out
And there was no doubt
The husband was a cheating rascal

Now Ace had the proof he needed
To tell her he had succeeded
"It was an affair,
but don't despair"
When confronted, the scoundrel conceded

It ended as expected, of course...
There was a quite bitter divorce
Although not funny
She got all the money
And for that she had no remorse!

So whenever he's put to the test
Ace always proves to be the best
The very next time
That there is a crime
Let him put your fears to rest

Not So Square

A carpenter, late one night
Found a corner that wasn't quite tight
When measured anew
He saw "one-oh-two"
An angle he knew wasn't "right"

Blundered Plunder

A cemetery crook named Jake
Tried to see how much he could take
He was bound to fail
And end up in jail
For he had made a grave mistake

Ewe Ought to Know Better

A crooked farmhand named Graham
Sought to profit from any scam
He met Ms. Bo Peep
Stole one of her sheep
And is now living life on the lamb

A Cast of One

Behold! Actor Bradford Bombillius
Plays his parts, perfectly punctilious
But oh, on his own
A new side is shown
His soliloquy style is the silliest

She took her self-defense course seriously!

So prepared was Miss Sally the smuggler,
When the circus troupe started a struggle, her
Cargo was sought
Though theft it was not…
For she stopped 'em – she went for the juggler!

Rick's Tricks

An unscrupulous poacher named Rick
Fished with a dynamite stick
Once his bait exploded
His live well was loaded
With any fish he wanted to pick

On seeing Rick make for the dock
The warden was in quite a shock
Rick tossed him lit bait
And told him "Don't wait!
You gonna fish, or stand there and talk?"

A map to the kitchen, please.

A real estate mogul in Boston
Never cared what houses were costin'
Because with his budget
He always said: "Fudge it!"
His homes he was always lost in

Ace Returns

Remember our detective named Ace?
He recently took a new case
A pretty thing
With lots of bling
Came traipsing into his place

"My name is Misses O'Malley"
She continued, "the first name is Sally.
My first directive:
Find a detective!
I've a problem that's right up your alley."

She sat down and heavily sighed
"I'm afraid my husband has died…
I'm all alone!
He isn't at home."
And then she broke down and cried

Then after a very good cry
She said "He's been secretive, I won't lie!
He oft sneaks around,
And is rarely found."
She asked Ace: "Perhaps he's a spy?"

Ace said, "As a matter of course…
I will check every single source!
I will follow each clue
Yes, that's what I do.
In the end, you will have no remorse."

Ace checked the CIA and INTERPOL,
The FBI and Man from U.N.C.L.E.,
And Hawaii Five-O
But none were a "go"
Espionage was an unlikely goal

Pausing from the investigation
At a trendy speakeasy location
Ace found the truth
Behind his vermouth
The missing man poured Ace's libation!

The enigmatic Mr. O'Malley
Then started for the kitchen (or galley)
Ace, on a whim
Called out: "You're him!
The man sought in each hill and valley."

O'Malley then returned to Ace
And he explained himself post-haste
"Despite what she thinks
I'm out slinging drinks
And I happily run my own place!"

It was very lucky that Ace
Had met with this man face to face
In this cool speakeasy
The answers came easy
And O'Malley asked Ace for more space

When next Ace and Sally did meet
Ace consoled her: "don't be downbeat…
Your husband's been found!
He's right here in town
At a speakeasy behind Main Street!"

"So dry your eyes; hubby's not dead.
He's not a spy - but a barkeep instead,"
Ace said from his chair.
"So please take care,
That the speakeasy password won't spread."

"Thank you, Ace, my mind is at ease!
Here's a check to cover your fees
Put to the test
You are the best
No one else has your expertise"

Ace said: "My work here is done!
It's time to go have some fun.
I'll head to the beach;
Cool drink within reach
As I sit and soak up the sun."

Conductive Conduct

A foolish man awoke to wonder:
"What if I flew a kite in thunder?"
Alas his poor luck
'Twas lightning that struck
And now he sleeps six feet under

A trick (or more) from Sycamore

A magician from Sycamore
Was asked for one more encore
It was quite a feat
He went down the street
And turned into a hardware store

Hanky-Panky Boogie

A magician just told me a secret
To make a hanky dance, just a bit
So, I'll tell you, too -
Here's what you do…
You put a little boogie in it

Travel Time

A slow boat to Thailand

Beaches like dear old Phuket's
Are far from Massachusetts
If comfort you need
On that long flight indeed
Just imagine that trip before jets

30,000 Feet of Shuteye

Whenever I board on a flight
I beam with a Zenlike delight
For with the din
Of a jet engine
I sleep better than in bed at night

No one else is holdin' back...

Ever caught a foul whiff on your bus?
The cause of transit odorous...
Is quick to explain;
People fart on the train.
So let loose and join the chorus!

I bet the apples won

Aboard a conveyance vehicular
On a trip extra-curricular
Some students, quite leery
Of Newton's theory
Raced their apples down the funicular

Well, it's just one city within the region, OK?

A finely dressed writer named Reese
Told me this, of her garments of fleece:
"I bought these pants
In the South of France."
So, I said: "Oh hey - that's Nice!"

GP-Guess

Two climbers, way up in the Alps
Were lost and scratchin' their scalps
One said: "I'm doubtin'
We're on the right mountain!
Check the map and see if that halps."

Wacky Waltzers

Two nudists from Battle Creek
Had been waltzing at least a week
To be profound
They turned around
And finished their dance cheek to cheek!

Hope they like the cold...

There was a young genius named Kris
Who loved a most beautiful miss
And after they wed
To the Arctic they fled
Where they live in connubial bliss!

Quintilla Jocosa

Molestado por un mosquito
Pensaba así un sapito
"Que suerte que tenga
Tanta gran lengua
Y su pico sea tan chiquito"

Reading, 'riting, 'rithmetic

Rhetorical Ramblings

For my peers, US and Australian
With tendencies sesquipedalian
One piece of advice:
"Be clear and concise"
Though this thought, I admit, may be alien

For mixed signals lead to frustration
And may hinder your eloquation.
The object is, surely
When transmitting, purely
To strive to eschew obfuscation

Whereas, heretofore, and thereunder
Your meaning has all gone asunder
You might try to distract
With big words to exact
New sense from your verbacious blunder

If a loquacious rant won't accrue
More sense than shorter words do
As a last resort
Sound off a "report"
Cover it up with a sneeze... achoo!

Shhhh...

Sometimes English words baffle me
They often cause us to disagree
Here's what I meant
Take the word "scent"
What's silent – the "s" or the "c"?

At least it's polite...

Count by Q: 1Q, 2Q, skip some
5Q, 6Q, this is kind of dumb,
8Q, then 9Q
We're almost through
And finally, 10Q! You're welcome!

Keep at it

A limerick is hard to write
It can take all day and all night
You've to rhyme
Every single time
But when finished, what a delight!

A few dollars and no sense

Limericks are meant to funny
We write ours to be quite "punny"
We will be proud
If you laugh out loud
But they sure won't make us any money

This limerick intentionally left blank

_ _ _ _ _ _ _ _ _
_ _ _ _ _ _ _ _ _
_ _ _ _ _
_ _ _ _ _
_ _ _ _ _ _ _ _ _

Got your words wrong

Is it pop or soda or coke?
Marshmallow fluff or cream? Puff or smoke?
Cart or Trolley?
Could be either, pro'ly
Please excuse me, if I've misspoke

Just don't cackle too loudly

Limericks are meant to be read
A great place to do this is in bed
Makes you smile
For a little while
'Ere sugar plums dance in your head

Family Matters

Wah-Wah-Wah

Once when one, wan, was Juan
When yon bon-bon was gone
Juan went "wah-wah"
While we saw Warsaw;
Juan's wont was warbling while wan

They must've moved a lot...

I rode the bus in my schoolboy days
and learnt of complaining - it never pays...
My folks and I talked;
They said they walked
For many miles — uphill — both ways!

Uncouth Youth

Advice to a young man named Dave;
When your first shave, you crave...
If you cut your lip...
Now *this* is the tip;
Don't ever put on aftershave!

Dads of Lads

There once were three rambunctious lads
Who wouldn't listen to their dads
Bad things await
For that's their fate
When sticking too close to comrades

Let's first take the lad named Ben
To his dad he didn't listen
Right around noon
He swallowed a spoon
And poor Ben never stirred again

The next to ignore dad was Billy
He wanted to do everything silly
He opened root beer
With the lobe of his ear
The result was of course, a wet willy

Lastly, a strong lad named Steve
Gave a boulder a vertical heave
In seeking to catch
Quickly met his match
Dad said: "'tis better to give than receive"

So, listen to your Pop, my son
His love for you is never done
Always be nice
Heed his advice
For one day, you may soon be one!

The Prices of Crises

When a man has finally turned fifty
And passed half his life being thrifty
He is struck by an urge
To spend it all! Splurge!
So will purchase a sports car so nifty

After buying his new convertible
He discovers an incontrovertible
Truth and/or fact
The car must go back!
Once its monthly cost is discernible

Reflections on Life

The Angels blew Gabriel's horn
And I was conceived one morn
In the womb I grew
As the time flew
And then one fine day I was born

As an infant I really liked to sleep
Mom and Pop would hold me a heap
At times I'd cry
I'm not sure why
They loved it when I made no peep

I learned to crawl and learned to eat
I cooed and made sounds sort of sweet
I'd roll side to side
I'd take a stride
My folks were so proud of each feat

A busy toddler I soon became
Activity was my middle name
I'd run and run
Having lots of fun
Everything was one big game

One day it was time for school
Mom thought me ready, despite my drool
Would it be fun?
When would it get done?
But I'll be a big kid, that's so cool!

I really enjoyed kindergarten
Got free books from Dolly Parton
Colors, scissors, glue
Even nap time too
My favorite was milk in a carton

First grade really was a delight
Learned to read and really got bright
Always got hot lunch
And liked it a bunch
Best of all, learned to be polite

In second grade, I learned to write
We got homework every night
Learned to spell
But not too well
And my penmanship was a fright

I learned an awful lot in grade three
Math, English, and History
I did quite well
As you can tell
My report card was all A's and a B

That brings us now to grade four
In which I learned even more
Some cursive writing
A little fighting
And girls I started to adore

The very best year was in fifth grade
I figured things out and had it made
Went by fast
And I passed
Now middle school, the next escapade

I thought middle school was quite rough
Social interactions were awkward and tough
Got teased a lot
I often fist fought
Couldn't wait to be done with this stuff

High school was a different story
I found myself in my glory
Academics, sports
Friends of all sorts
Ready to create my place in history

In college I made my folks very proud
Studied hard – no failure allowed
I'd ace a test
That was the best
And I graduated Summa Cum Laude

I soon entered the rat race
I worked hard and earned my place
It was a blast
Moved up fast
A work hard, play hard paper chase

I started dating a fine young miss
The earth shook at our first kiss
I asked her to marry
She said, "why tarry?"
And we entered into wedded bliss

Soon the pitter patter of little feet
Showed me that kids are a treat
A girl and boy
Brought us great joy
A parent's job is never complete

I worked forty years then did I retire!
Now there's hobbies and grandkids I admire
There's no more rat race!
Go at your own pace
These are the best days of my life entire

When I am finally old and gray
I'll look back and appreciate each day
Family and friends
From beginning to end
Made life a blessing in every way

When I go, think of me; don't be sad
This life was the best one ever had
I hope that you'll smile
And laugh a while
Know that your love made me glad

Gaming the System

No more Mr. Nice Guy

A chess master moving his queen
Said he did not want to be mean
But he's not to blame
If he wins every game
He's been playing since he was a teen!

You might try developing it earlier

A chess player moving his knight
Was trying to put up a fight
But still to his shame
He lost every game
There's something he's not doing right!

Losers have easier cleanup!

A young novice moving her pawn
Liked playing chess out on the lawn
When the game was done
Her opponent had won
And all of her pieces were gone!

Maybe she should switch to SCRABBLE

A bewildered young woman debated
To play chess, a game that she hated
She didn't give thought
To her moves like she ought
And so she was quickly checkmated!

SCRABBLE can be tough, too!

A new SCRABBLE-r went through a phase
She'd lost every game in 10 days
She said without smiles,
As she turned in her tiles,
"I can't make a word with six A's!"

Then there's a triple-letter score on that 'Z'

A SCRABBLE whiz couldn't be beat
Sent her rivals to utter defeat
At the end of her game
She was able to claim
She'd played both "muzjik" and "mesquite"

Note: "muzjik" refers to a Russian Peasant; letter tiles Q, Z, J, and K have high point values

Go big AND go home...

A bridge player got in a jam
By bidding an unwise grand slam
And now he's in debt
By six tricks was he set
And said "Oh, the fool I am!"

Celebrities and Characters

But they're all good at 'Family Feud'

The Magnificent Miss Meghan Markle
Entranced the world with her sparkle
Fortune, I suppose
Favors her throws
Of the dice - in life and at Farkle

Soon after becoming Duchess
Meghan issued a Royal address
To proclaim affection
For the game "Perfection"
And classics like Checkers and Chess

This made her new in-laws uneasy
In fact they were downright queasy
You see the Queen
Was always quite keen
To maintain her reign at Parcheesi

The approval of her newest daughter
Like a Jenga tower did totter
When games did begin
"Meg" let the queen win
Just like a good Duchess oughter

Pronounce it like the Queen...

A young Miss Demi Lovato
Was dining on boiled potato
A sudden mishap
Put some in her lap
And her face went red as a tomato

Mixed Massages

The hardworking Arianna Grande
Who sought to relax after a long day
She called a masseuse
To make muscles loose
But alas, they rubbed her the wrong way

Fear of Missing Out

The provocative Miss Kim Kardashian
Famous for feats of high Fashian
Does she seek limelight
From FOMO-ish fright?
Or is it truly her Pashian?

A Treat to Meet

I love the music of Billy Joel
To meet him would be my goal
I'm a huge fan
Of the piano man
It would be beneficial for my soul

Dig Your Own Party Favor

Olympics announcer Bob Costas
To a potluck, brought over some pastas
The night's end drew near,
He 'dug' a souvenir;
Mr. Costas stole one of our hostas

Capricious Crockett

Once when dear old Davy Crockett
Found a hole in his breast pocket
He traded that shirt
For a denim skirt
Then said: "'til you've tried it, don't knock it!"

Wardrobe Malfunction

When that Twin, dear old Kirby Puckett
Had a big uniform run amuck, it
Near his knees did approach
So he asked his coach:
"Hey, could you please help me tuck it?"

Never Lend Livestock

Ms. Bo Peep, played by Helen Mirin
Will be, in a new film, appearin'
Where her ewe is leased
Then thoroughly "fleeced"
By a conman played by Ed Sheeran

Late Night

Most nights I watch the Tonight show
Jimmy Fallon hosts, as you might know
He's quick with a smile
And I like his style
But the best was always Jay Leno

There's O'Brien, Corden, and Colbert
And Myers and Kimmell are both fair
Very good folks
With lots of jokes
But by far Leno had the most flair

For five years now, he's been retired
Even so he is still very admired
His silly grin
His funny chin
But now it's Fallon that's desired

Holidazed

Hate to be his dentist...

There once was a man who was born
In the twilight of Hallow's eve morn
His looks were som'thin!
For his head, a pumpkin
His grin was made of candy corn

Counting Calories, Count?

Dracula, on the scale, late one night
Exclaimed: "My weight is quite a fright!
I'll fix this, somehow…
and cut back, right now
From now on, I drink only Blood Lite!"

For good health, the Count knows a trick:
Eat nothing that contains garlic
And for heaven's sake
Never touch a 'steak'
And be careful with a wooden toothpick!

Pre-diet, Count Drac' was a fatty
He was pallid, and paunchy, and ratty
Since losing the weight
Old Vlad's feeling great
But I hear he still acts a bit batty

Holy Matri-moly

A romantic spirit named Lance
Once wooed a young specter of France
She quickly said: "No!"
And bade him to go
For he hadn't a ghost of a chance

Not to be dismissed out of hand
He hired a thirteen-piece band
And as they played
Her cold heart was swayed
For their songs (and piano) were grand

Although the prospect was daunting
Lance got the outcome he was wanting
The change was profound
When she came around
To join Lance in an amorous haunting

Dressed up, all glow-y and blanch-y
At a graveyard, all brambly and branchy
By the light of the moon
They danced to a tune
Wailed by a brusque-sounding banshee

T'was then that Lance made his plea
To propose that they forever be
She said: "Since we're dead,
We ought to be wed!
I guess that the spirit moved me."

Their wedding was festive but queer
The guests gave them toasts and three cheers
The bride was a fright
So vested in white
And even the cake was in tiers

Years flew by, and they had a chat
About hearing some feet pitter pat
Ten ghostlings in all
Coasting through the hall
But they sure weren't much to look at

Just don't sleep through dessert!

Thanksgiving is time for turkey
Stuffing brown, and gravy murky
At meal's end, mayhap
Go and take a nap
And enjoy the day off from work-y

Waiting out a winter wonderland...

Is there any time quite like the Yule?
The kids all get let out of school
Despite holly and snow
We can't wait to go
Any place with some sun and a pool

A hemisphere not far from here...

When cold and snow long assail ya
And you long to shed winter regalia
You should remember
That mid-December
Is summertime down in Australia

Why not set the bar lower?

Late December: a time oft deplored
We resolve things we can ill-afford
We swear, first of Jan
To enact our new plan
By the second, our scheme is ignored

Better lend him a scarf!

Cold, wind, and snow have one merit:
Misery! (we all seem to share it)
My hands and lips chap
With every cold snap;
Our snowman has a frostbitten carrot

Nothing says "love" like an orbital sander...

Mid-June is a time when we stop
To accessorize a toolbox or shop
On Fathers' day
We all try to say
"You're the best - we love you, Pop!"

Who invited them anyway?

Who doesn't love the Fourth of July?
Summer heat, fireworks, apple pie
We enjoy all the guests
But perennial pests
Like the mosquito and biting fly

Peal the Bells

A gentleman called Barry McGarry
Met a merry young lass, named Mary
In a little while
He'll walk down the aisle
Merry Mary and Barry McGarry will marry

Madcap Menagerie

Peculiar Pelican't

"It's impossible! Never happen! It shan't!"
Cried the big billed bird on a rant
"It won't, it won't!
I don't, I don't!"
Wailed the pessimistic Pelican't

The Pelican't is a very strange bird
Everything he does is quite absurd
If things are great
He'll still be irate
And always have a negative word

When served a nice dinner of bass
He rejects it and requests some wrasse
His negative mood
Is outlandishly rude
And his manners devoid of all class

His sharp tongue never does rest
When critiquing the way one is dressed
He'll insult your hat
And show off his cravat
To flaunt how his chest wears it best

What can be done with a bird so queer?
How do you stop his rant insincere?
Turn him upside down
Twist his frown around
And make sure he grins ear to ear

Fetch him a large cup of coffee
And ask him to trade for his "t"
Without that letter
A Pelican't is much better
For now a Pelican will he be

When you find a Pelican't rattling cages
Smile, be polite, and courageous;
A nice salutation
And warm affirmation
Do a lot - good moods are contagious!

Please don't laugh at my calf...

A two-humped camel named Ali
Married a one hump camel named Brie
They then had a son;
No hump on this one…
So they named their baby Humphrey!

Your wipers will just make it worse...

One evening an insect named Pete
Flew down a fast-moving street
He suddenly crashed
His memories flashed
The last thing through his mind were his feet

Priorities are important!

An oversized house cat named Snap
Continued to sit on my lap
When told: "there's a mouse
That's loose in the house!"
Said, "I'd rather be taking a nap."

Bet that crown slows him down

In the crows nest, atop the ship sails
Capt. Ahab withstood windy gales
To be on lookout
For a glint and spout
The telltales of the crown prince of whales

Too bad it wasn't a Beatle

When a textile worker of Wemyss
Stopped serging to inspect some seams
She saw a beetle
Atop her needle
And the factory was filled with her screams

Crooked Croc

I once saw an alligator smile
He sneered; he was very hostile
He caused me some grief…
He robbed me. That thief!
Not a gator; but a crook-o-dile.

Hope there was mint jelly...

There once was a weepy old lion
Who met a new lamb from Zion
That tender young sheep
Took one naive leap
And gave him a shoulder to cry on

The 'wash in Oshkosh

A farmer down in Oshkosh
Cleaned off some swine and some squash
Those veggies, I think,
Were rinsed in the sink
The pigs she sent through the hogwash

Can't teach an old hog new tricks

An old hog - a real smarty pants
Thought to try the art of breakdance
Though he spun around
Three times on the ground
He left in the ham-bulance

Pondering Porkchops

So masterfully made is the pig!
A fair flavor with fennel or fig
Or here's another;
Add gravy and smother
With mushrooms and a rosemary sprig

But I bet it tastes 'lighter'

One morning, while passing a sty
I pondered: "What if pigs could fly?"
It later came true!
At that time I knew:
It means bacon prices go sky high!

Eight arms can work a lot of fryers!

A spider's new food enterprise
Moved to a drive-through franchise
Working the fryer
She spun an empire
Of hambuggers with sides of french flies

Amphibian Refreshment

The frogs that live at Loyola
Eat bugs atop Gorgonzola
Then have a drink -
You'll know it, I think -
They swig an ice-cold Croak-a-Cola

Hop to it!

The frog is not dull! That's misplaced.
Their spare time rarely goes to waste
They attend the Hop-era
Or read Deepak Chopra
In fact, they've got quite new-age tastes

Before the show are the pre-moos

A young cow by the name of Louise
Asked a mate: "For a date, if you please?"
I suppose you will know
Where two cows would go...
Of course, they went to the moo-vies!

Should've got a running start...

A nimble momma cow did decree:
"I'll jump a fence that's four-foot three!"
I'm sad to report
That she came up short
It was an udder catastrophe

Sharing is Caring

A large herd from dear old Khartoum
Munched on some clover in bloom
One cow couldn't move
Cried: "I disapprove!
Moo-ve over and give me some room."

DIY Lawncare

A cow whose yard was much newer
Had grass that was just a shade bluer
It needed a cut
She used her… guess what?
She fired up her good old lawn moo-er!

Early to bed...

A momma cow down in Anaheim
Said: "Kids, your behavior is a crime!
Now, go to sleep.
And without a peep!
It is way, way pasture bedtime"

This zoo has a museum, too.

At the zoo they keep Bovine and Bre-am
Other animals, too - go see 'em!
The fish are in tanks
No touching, please? Thanks.
And the cows are kept in the moo-seum

But can it moo-ltiply?

A farmer - a modern operator
Had to tally his herd now or later
Not one for counting
When sums were mounting
He pulled out his cow-culator

Passing the Bar

O'Malley's Sallies

In a bar called O'Malley's place
Came a horse who just lost his race
He asked for: "a brew...
Or maybe a few"
"Coming up! But why the long face?"

Although this tale may sound queer
O'Malley never lies, my dear
A termite walked in
With a sheepish grin
And asked, "is the bar tender here?"

And just as the bar was closing
Two jumper cables were moseying
"Can we come in?"
They asked with a grin.
"You can - but don't start anything!"

Then in walks a neutron named Marge
Who ran up a bill, quite large
"I've got to go -
What do I owe?"
"For you my dear, there is no charge"

Three runners: Larry, Robert, and Chuck
Sought a bar, for to drown their bad luck
By the light of a star
Two ran into the bar
But alas, the third chose to duck

There came a grasshopper, one eve
Which O'Malley found hard to believe
"We've a drink, I confess…
Named for your likeness"
"That's weird! Why'd you call a drink Steve?"

The notes "C", "E-flat" and "G"
Asked O'Malley for a whiskey
He said, "Go away!
You cannot stay.
For I never serve minors, you see."

One evening, uncomfortably hot
Descartes walked in to the spot
When asked, "while you're here,
How 'bout a cold beer?"
He disappeared once he said, "I think not!"

Next into that bar was a toad
With asphalt, underarm, for his load
He shouted "A brew!
"Wait, make it two.
One for me and one for the road!"

A man's lexicographical flaw
Has him down to his very last straw
So when he thinks
To imbibe some drinks
The dyslexic man goes to the bra

A duck waddled in late one Fall
And requested "some grapes, that is all!"
"No grapes here!"
O'Malley did sneer
"Ask again, I'll nail your beak to the wall!"

The duck returned shaking its tail
And this time, asked to purchase a nail
Said O'Malley: "There's none."
And the duck replied "Fun!
Have you got any grapes for sale?"

Skunk, Frog, and Giraffe wanted beer
So they barged in the place, cavalier.
They had drinks aplenty;
Their tab was two-twenty!
But how to pay, well, that was unclear...

Says Skunk, "I've just one 'cent,' you see...
And Frog's 'greenback' is too small, you'll agree"
Then up pipes Giraffe
(With a big laugh)
"I guess you'll both need a 'spot' from me!"

So come hobnob with O'Malley's gentry
And take in the humor element'ry
Here the half-wits
Will leave you in fits
But hey - the nuts are compliment'ry

Sleep Deep

In my basement I like to make wine
It almost always turns out fine
If I drink red
And go to bed
My dreams are simply divine

And if I decide to drink white
My dreams are quite a delight
So, go ahead
Imbibe before bed
Red or white, you'll have a goodnight

Bonus Content

A Request for the Reader

You've now read our whole book, it's true
Whatever are we going to do?
Although it's done,
We sure had fun.
And sincerely hope that you did, too!

So now that we must say 'goodbye'
Could you please go and rate us high?
Tell Amazon.com
Or even your mom!
And perhaps incent more folks to buy

The book is now really at its end
You've read the best that we've penned
So before we go
We want you to know
We thank you for reading, dear friend

More Books by these Authors

Enjoyed this, and hungry for more?

Search "Lovable Limericks" on the Kindle Store.

Made in the USA
Columbia, SC
30 November 2023